ORTHODOX THEOLOGY
IN THE TWENTY-FIRST CENTURY

DOXA & PRAXIS
Exploring Orthodox Theology

Dr PANTELIS KALAITZIDIS, *series editor*

In light of the current challenges faced by global Christianity, Doxa & Praxis, a collaborative effort of the Volos Academy and WCC Publications, invites creative and original reflection that reappraises, reappropriates and further develops the riches of Orthodox thought for a deep renewal of Orthodox Christianity and for the benefit of the whole oikoumene.

Board of Editorial Consultants

METROPOLITAN
KALLISTOS WARE

ORTHODOX THEOLOGY
IN THE TWENTY-FIRST CENTURY

Foreword by
PANTELIS KALAITZIDIS

**World Council
of Churches**
Publications

ORTHODOX THEOLOGY
IN THE TWENTY-FIRST CENTURY
Doxa & Praxis series

WCC Publications is the book publishing programme of the World Council of Churches. Founded in 1948, the WCC promotes Christian unity in faith, witness and service for a just and peaceful world. A global fellowship, the WCC brings together more than 349 Protestant, Orthodox, Anglican and other churches representing more than 560 million Christians in 110 countries and works cooperatively with the Roman Catholic Church.

Opinions expressed in WCC Publications are those of the authors.

Scripture quotations are from the New Revised Standard Version Bible, © copyright 1989 by the Division of Christian Education of the National Council of the Churches of Christ in the USA. Used by permission.

Book design and typesetting: Indiktos Publications, Athens Greece
ISBN: 978-2-8254-1571-9

World Council of Churches
150 route de Ferney, P.O. Box 2100
1211 Geneva 2, Switzerland
http://publications.oikoumene.org

CONTENTS

FOREWORD
Pantelis Kalaitzidis*

O ver the last several decades, Orthodoxy has been experi-
encing a creative and fruitful theological and ecclesial
renewal, which is taking place in various contexts within the
Orthodox world, in spite of some painful changes and the
temptation of introversion. In our current post-secular age,
Orthodoxy defines itself not as a besieged fortress or a defensive
stronghold but as a genuine liberating message and rejuvenating
spiritual experience, faithful to its apostolic roots and ecumenical
vocation and ready to respond to the existential needs of humanity
with its "words of eternal life" (cf. Jn. 6:68). The recent ferment
in and growing influence of Orthodox theology have indeed
led to wider appreciation of the strength and the richness of
Orthodox tradition. Specifically in light of the current challenges
faced by global Christianity, we are invited to a creative and
original reflection that reappraises, reappropriates, and further
develops the riches of Orthodox thought and insights for a deep
renewal of Orthodox Christianity and for the benefit of the
whole *oikoumene*. This is precisely the goal and the main concern
of this new series, Doxa & Praxis: Exploring Orthodox Theology,
a collaborative effort of the Volos Academy, Volos, Greece, and
WCC Publications, Geneva.

We could not imagine a better beginning for this new series than
this book by Metropolitan Kallistos Ware on *Orthodox Theology
in Twenty-first Century*, which comes out of the Volos Academy's

* Dr Pantelis Kalaitzidis, editor of the series Doxa & Praxis: Exploring Orthodox Theology, is Director of the Volos Academy for Theological Studies, Volos, Greece.

series of public lectures. Faithful to its founding principle, which defines it as "an open forum of thought and dialogue between the Orthodox Church and the broader scholarly community of intellectuals worldwide, without defensive attitude or apologetic mind," the Volos Academy for Theological Studies of the Holy Metropolis of Demetrias, in Volos, Greece, during the academic year 2003-2004, through a self-critical and open-minded discourse, attempted to raise timely and vital issues in the Orthodox ecclesial and theological self-consciousness. Thus, after the series of public lectures, seminars, and international conferences on *Church and Eschatology; Orthodoxy and Modernity; Gender and Religion–The Role of Women in the Orthodox Church; Islam and Fundamentalism–Orthodox Christianity and Globalization; Theology and Modern Literature; Theology and Contemporary Church Architecture,* and before the Volos Academy's well-known international conferences on *Forgiveness, Reconciliation and Peace; Turmoil in Post-war Theology: The Greek "Theology of the '60s"; Eucharist, Church, and the World; The Participation of Orthodox Women in the Ecumenical Movement; Church and Culture; Biblical Liberation Theology, Patristic Theology, and the Ambivalences of Modernity; Neo-Patristic Synthesis or Post-Patristic Theology: Can Orthodox Theology Be Contextual?; Christian Presence and Witness in Palestine and the Middle East Today: Theological and Political Challenges,* and more, the Volos Academy dedicated its 2003-2004 program to the study of the issue of *Orthodoxy and Multiculturalism.* It was ground-breaking for Orthodox theology. The importance and the timeliness of this topic, both for the Orthodox Church and its theology as well as for the so-called traditionally Orthodox societies cannot be underestimated.

In fact, as was pointed out by many of the speakers of the

program on *Orthodoxy and Multiculturalism*,[1] the challenge of globalization and the reality of multicultural societies, with the osmosis of populations, cultures, and religions, urgently raise the question of religious otherness, the relation with the "other," who images the "Other" par excellence. The appearance and consolidation of many types of "otherness" (national, religious, ideological, social, age-based, etc.) in the lives of peoples and societies has led to the loss of a homogeneous social and religious space and to the radical transformation of closed traditional societies into something new. Economic development, information technology and the communication revolution, rapid geopolitical changes, and the consequent demographic population movements have brought about a radical amalgamation of peoples and a cultural osmosis. These factors make the demand for religious co-existence and dialogue between cultures an urgent matter, while at the same time pointing out the danger of religious syncretism–leaving always open, however, the call to evangelism and mission–and calling the Orthodox Church to become aware of the above changes, and to prepare itself for an appropriate theological and pastoral answer to them.

If multiculturalism and otherness represent the first great challenge for Orthodoxy today, the rapid progress of science and the biotechnology revolution–which radically changed the playing field in anthropology and bioethics–represent another equally important challenge. It is to this "other" challenge that His Eminence, Metropolitan of Diokleia Kallistos Ware (Ecu-

---

1. See the volume P. Kalaitzidis-N. Asproulis, eds., *Orthodoxy and Multiculturalism*, Volos Academy series of public lectures 2003-04 (Volos: Academy of Demetrias Publications, 2012) [in Greek].

menical Patriarchate)–former Spalding Lecturer in Eastern Orthodox Studies at Oxford University and presently Emeritus Fellow of Pembroke College, Oxford–aims to respond in this lecture. Metropolitan Kallistos, one of the pre-eminent theological and ecclesiastical figures of our time, gave his public lecture in Volos, Greece, on *Orthodox Theology in the Twenty-first Century*, in the framework of the program on *Orthodoxy and Multiculturalism*, on April 28, 2004, in front of a packed audience that turned out not only from the city of Volos but from other parts of Greece as well, all of whom came to hear and meet with this distinguished hierarch and theologian.

The dominant motif of Metropolitan Kallistos Ware's lecture is the thesis that while, during the twentieth century, the primary theological issue was ecclesiological – that is, the problem of the identity and the nature of the Church–in the twenty-first century, in light of rapid developments in science and information technology, environmental biotechnology, environmental ethics and bioethics, the quintessential problem for Orthodox theology will be the anthropological. The conditions and possibilities of dialogue between Orthodox theology, first with its past and with its ecclesiological/eucharistic self-consciousness, and then with the challenges of ecology, genetic engineering, biotechnology and modern anthropology, represent the major challenges outlined in this short but rich text. Its thematic autonomy in regard to the remaining papers of the series of public lectures on *Orthodoxy and Multiculturalism* is the main reason for this separate publication.

Before concluding this Foreword, let me extend warm thanks to His Eminence, Metropolitan Kallistos Ware of Diokleia, both for honoring us by accepting the Volos Academy's invitation to deliver his public lecture and for his kindness in giving us permission to publish it as a book, first in Greek and now in English. For the Volos Academy and WCC Publications, it is truly a privilege and blessing to start this new joint series, Doxa & Praxis: Exploring Orthodox Theology, with this brilliant text, which says much and promises much more for the future and rejuvenation of Orthodox theology in the twenty-first century. Sincere thanks is also due to the Manager of WCC Publications, Mr. Michael West, for his continual support and encouragement, and his vital contribution to the preparation and launch of this new joint series Doxa & Praxis: Exploring Orthodox Theology.

ORTHODOX THEOLOGY
IN THE TWENTY-FIRST CENTURY

Chapter 1
LOOKING TO THE PAST:
OUR CHIEF TASK IN THE TWENTIETH CENTURY

Let us begin by asking ourselves a double question, of crucial relevance to our situation as Orthodox Christians facing the cultural diversity and pluralism of the contemporary world. What has been the principal issue confronting Orthodox theology during the century that has just drawn to a close? And what will be the principal issue before us during the new millennium, as we embark upon the twenty-first century? Manifestly this double question can be approached from many different points of view, and others will certainly disagree with my order of priorities.

For myself, I see the dominant theme in Orthodox theology during the past century as *ecclesiology*. Indeed, well before the dawn of the twentieth century, in the 1840s and 1850s, the problem of the essential nature of the Church had already been raised in Russia by Slavophiles such as Aleksei Khomiakov. They were seeking to identify the distinctive character of Orthodoxy, as contrasted with Roman Catholicism on the one side and with Protestantism on the other; and this led them to insist, in their vision of the Church, upon the primacy of love over power. It is here, in their concern to liberate ecclesiology from juridical categories, that they made their most characteristic and enduring contribution to Orthodox thinking. That which holds the Church together, so they insisted, is not power of jurisdiction but mutual love. As Khomiakov affirmed, "The knowledge of the truth is given to mutual love." By virtue of this mutual love, the Church, in its *sobornost* or collegial catholicity, is a living miracle of free unanimity. In the Church, and in it alone, mutual love –after the likeness of the eternal *perichoresis* or movement of reciprocal indwelling within the Holy Trinity – effects a genuine reconciliation between liberty and unity.

During the twentieth century this question of the essential nature of the Church was posed in the Orthodox world with fresh urgency. This was above all for two reasons. The first reason was the collapse of the Russian Empire in 1917, followed by the Bolshevik persecution of Christianity. Hitherto the Russian Orthodox Church had been closely integrated into the total structure of the state and nation, enjoying as a matter of course a privileged status at every level, whether politically, economically or in the realm of education. As a result of the 1917 revolution, the Constantinian *symphonia* between Church and state had been abruptly terminated, and this sudden change led Russians and other Orthodox to ask themselves: What is the Church here for? If it ceases to be a national or state institution, what then is its distinctive function? What does it do that nobody and nothing else can do? Moreover, if the ecclesiastical hierarchy no longer has any support from the civil authorities, what holds the Church together and maintains it in unity?

A second factor that brought to the forefront the question of ecclesiology was the widespread emigration of Orthodox Christians to the West (this, indeed, was partly the direct result of the first factor, the Russian revolution). Dwelling as a small minority among non-Orthodox Christians, Greeks, Russians, Arabs and others were challenged to give an account of their distinctive self-understanding as Orthodox; and this challenge was compounded by their growing involvement in the ecumenical movement. Once more as Orthodox we were obliged to ask ourselves: What is the Church here for? What do we as members of the Orthodox Church share with Western Christians, and what makes us different? What have we to teach the non-Orthodox, and what have we to learn from them?

To this question, "Why the Church?" a one-sided yet prophetic answer was given by Archpriest Nikolai Afanassieff, who had been brought up in imperial Russia but was driven into exile in 1920, settling first in Serbia and then in Paris.[2] In his search for the essential meaning of the Church, he looked back, behind the conversion of the Emperor Constantine and the "establishment" of Christendom in the fourth century, to the situation of the pre-Nicene Christianity. Appealing to the ecclesiology of St Ignatius of Antioch, he emphasized the fundamental bond between Church and the Eucharist. The Church, he maintained, is primarily a eucharistic organism, which becomes authentically itself when, and only when, it celebrates the Divine Liturgy. The distinctive and primary function of the Church is to celebrate the Lord's Supper, the Messianic banquet of the age to come, until Christ returns (1 Cor. 11:26). Ecclesial unity is not imposed from above by power of jurisdiction but created from within through sharing in the Saviour's body and blood. It is Holy Communion that holds the Church together: "We who are many are one body, because we all partake of the one loaf" (1 Cor. 10:17). The Eucharist constitutes, in a fallen and sinful world, the life-giving source of all the Church's social, cultural and educational work. Without the Eucharist there would be no Church. The Church makes the Eucharist, and the Eucharist makes the Church. The Church is not a department of state but the place in which the Mystical Sacrifice is offered; its determining principle is not national or ethnic but sacramental.

Such was the theology of the Church that Afanassieff advanced in his celebrated essay, "The Church Which Presides in Love," published in French in 1960 and in English in 1963,[3] pre-

2. On Afanassieff, see Aidan Nichols, *Theology in the Russian Diaspora: Church, Fathers, Eucharist in Nikolai Afanas'ev (1893-1966)* (Cambridge: University Press, 1989).

3. In John Meyendorff (ed), *The Primacy of Peter,* new edition (Crestwood, N.Y.: St Vladimir's Seminary Press, 1992), pp. 91-143.

senting ideas that he had first developed thirty years earlier. In this way he re-emphasized the basic intuition of the Slavophiles that the Church is held together by mutual love. But, whereas the Slavophiles had taken as their model for organic unity the Russian peasant commune, Afanassieff gave a greater clarity and cogency to their standpoint by affirming a model that was not sociological but mysterial. Mutual love, he insisted –in a way that the Slavophiles had failed to do – is essentially eucharistic in character. The love that holds the Church together is not just an inner subjective feeling but has as its basis an objective act, the joint participation of Christians in Holy Communion.

In thus underlining the eucharistic nature of the Church, Afanassieff brought to the forefront its all-embracing character, as a reality that transcends national and cultural boundaries. The Slavophiles, by taking as their model the Russian peasant commune, had consciously and deliberately given to their ecclesiology a specifically Slav ethos. The catholicity (*sobornost)* of the Church, in their view, found its truest and fullest expression in Holy Russia. Afanassieff, on the other hand, by taking as his model the Eucharist, was no longer thinking in terms of Russian ethnicity. For in Christ Jesus "there is no longer Jew or Greek"(Gal. 3:28). And so in the Eucharist, as the sacrament of Christ's body and blood, divisions of race or nationality are surmounted; meeting around the Lord's table, we are all one. Eucharistic ecclesiology, then, is particularly appropriate to our Christian situation in the contemporary world, living as we do in a *milieu* that to an ever-increasing extent is multicultural and supranational.

Independently of Afanassieff for the most part, other Russian *émigré* theologians – most notably Archpriest Sergei Bulgakov and Archpriest Georges Florovsky – also recognized the essential connection between Church and Eucharist. For Florovsky, the Church is above all the Body of Christ; and he has well aware of the double meaning of the term "Body of Christ", signifying as it does both the sacrament of the Eucharist and the community of the Church.

Among Greek Orthodox theologians the eucharistic understanding of the Church has been systematically developed by John Zizioulas, Metropolitan of Pergamon, who has deepened and moderated Afanasssieff's approach, providing it with a more exact Patristic basis. In particular he questions the sharp contrast made by Afanassieff between "eucharistic" and "universal" ecclesiology. Metropolitan John points out that the Eucharist exists, not in isolation, but within a context that is both doctrinal and hierarchical. It is not enough to state, in unqualified terms, "The Eucharist makes the Church." It is necessary to add: The Church is present in its fullness only in that Eucharist at which the true faith is proclaimed, and which meets under the presidency of the bishop or with his blessing. Moreover, each local Church, as it celebrates the Eucharist, does so in communion with all the other local Churches throughout the world. The "eucharistic" and the "universal" understandings of the Church are thus not alternatives but complementary, and both "models" have a place in a balanced ecclesiology. In short, Afanassieff has over-emphasized the local aspect of the Church.[4]

4. See John D. Zizioulas, *Eucharist, Bishop, Church: The Unity of the Church in the Divine Eucharist and the Bishop during the First Three Centuries* (Brookline, Mass.: Holy Cross Orthodox Press, 2001), originally published in Greek in 1965; also *Being as Communion: Studies in Personhood and the Church* (London: Darton, Longman & Todd, 1985), especially pp.123-260. The best study of Zizioulas is Paul McPartlan, *The Eucharist Makes the Church: Henri de Lubac and John Zizioulas in Dialogue* (Edinburgh: T&T Clark, 1993).

Fortunately this eucharistic vision of the Church has not remained during the twentieth century merely an abstract theory, but its emergence has been accompanied by a revival of frequent communion in many Orthodox parishes (although, alas, not by any means in all). This is surely important. A eucharistic ecclesiology that is not reflected in the actual practice of the faithful would be unrealistic and even hypocritical. In the revival of frequent communion, a pioneering role was played in pre-revolutionary Russia by St John of Kronstadt. I recall his words each time that I celebrate the Liturgy: "The Eucharist is a continual miracle."

Such, then, is my answer to the first part of my question: the principal theological issue in twentieth-century Orthodoxy has been ecclesiology. It is, of course, no more than a partial answer. Another vitally important development in recent Orthodox theology has been the rediscovery of hesychast spirituality, the renewed interest in St Symeon the New Theologian and St Gregory Palamas, and the ever-increasing influence of *The Philokalia*. Here a leading part has been played by the Russians Vladimir Lossky, Archbishop Basil Krivocheine, and Archpriest John Meyendorff, by the Greeks George Mantzarides, Panagiotis Christou and Protopresbyter John Romanides and by the Romanian Archpriest Dumitru Staniloae. Nonetheless I see the past century as *par excellence* ecclesiological in its orientation.

CHAPTER 2
THE CHALLENGE OF THE NEW MILLENNIUM

It is time to turn to the second half of our double question. What will be the dominant theological *leitmotif* in the new century on which we are now embarking? I make no claim to be a prophet, but here is my own answer. In the twenty-first century, undoubtedly ecclesiology will continue to absorb our attention. It is my conviction, however, that there will be a shift in the central focus of theological inquiry from ecclesiology to anthropology; indeed, there are many signs that such a shift has already begun. The key question will be, not only, "What is the Church?" but also and more fundamentally, "What is the human person?" What does it mean, more specifically, to be a person-in-relation according to the image of God the Holy Trinity? Obviously there is an integral link between the two questions, "What is the Church?" and "What is the human person?"; for it is only in the Church that human persons become authentically themselves.

There are at least four connected reasons why this question concerning personhood is especially timely at the present moment. First, on the social and political level, we live in an era of ever-advancing urbanization and globalization. The individual, in his or her distinctive identity, is in danger of being swallowed up in blocks of flats, in vast housing estates, in complex international corporations. In itself the cultural pluralism that results from this globalization is an opportunity and a potential enrichment, not a disaster. Yet globalization can at the same time lead to the kind of collectivism in which personal diversity is obliterated. In such a situation it is essential to reaffirm the uniqueness and infinite value of each specific human being. We need to recall how in the age to come the righteous will be given "a white stone, and on the white stone is written a new name that no one knows except the one who receives it" (Rev. 2:17). We are each of us different, and in each there is to be found a treasure not given to anyone else; and this diversity will continue to all eternity. Our concern, as politicians, social scientists or church leaders, is not just with featureless conglomerations of human beings but much more fundamentally with particular persons, each of whom is unrepeatable and unpredictable.

In the second place, on the level of technology we are living in an age that is increasingly dominated by machines. My university colleagues are so busy talking to their computers that they have less and less time to talk to one another. Confronted by this dehumanizing tendency, there is an urgent need for us as Orthodox, and as Christians, to proclaim the supreme importance of direct encounter, person to person, face to face. It is no coincidence that the Greek word for person, *prosopon,* means precisely "countenance" or "face." I am genuinely personal only if I face others, if I enter into dialogue with them, if I look into their eyes and allow them to look into mine. In other words, today more than ever before it is vitally important to emphasize the value of friendship and personal love. Only persons are capable of love: you may love your computer, but your computer does not love you. We must not allow persons, with their astonishing capacity for mutual affection, to be overshadowed and engulfed by machines.

Thirdly, on the ethical level, recent developments in genetic engineering are raising problematic issues that, less than a generation ago, most of us had not even begun to think about. This has been accompanied by a widespread breakdown of the institution of marriage and a growing rejection of traditional sexual morality. As Orthodox, and as Christians, we cannot respond effectively to these challenges without a courageous and imaginative revitalization of our doctrine of human personhood.

Nor is this all. There is in the fourth place the disastrous ecological tragedy which, as the British Orthodox writer Philip Sherrard has effectively shown,[5] is directly related to our appreciation of what it is to be human. The tragedy is due, that is to say, not primarily to a crisis in the physical environment as such but to a crisis in the human heart, an anthropological crisis; for the basic problem is not merely technological or economic but, much more profoundly, personal and spiritual. If we are destroying the forests and the wild animals, and if we are rendering poisonous the air that we breathe and the water that we drink, that is because we have forgotten our authentic human identity, our true relation as human beings to the material world and our supreme human vocation as priests of God's creation. Our world image has been distorted because our human image, our self-understanding, has become fatally flawed. What is basically at fault is not our scientific skills but our theology of personhood, or rather our lack of such theology.

My own sense of human responsibility toward nature was strikingly enhanced, some forty-five years ago, when I was a deacon at the monastery of St John the Theologian on Patmos, where I came to know the spiritual father of the island, Archimandrite Amphilochios (Makris). He had a particular affection for trees. "Do you know," he used to say, "that God gave us one more commandment, which is not recorded in Scripture? It is the commandment *Love the trees.*" Whoever does not love trees, he was convinced, does not love Christ. "When you plant a tree," he told

---

5. See in particular his books *The Rape of Man and Nature: An Enquiry into the Origins and Consequences of Modern Science* (Ipswich: Golgonooza Press, 1987); *Human Image: World Image. The Death and Resurrection of Sacred Cosmology* (Ipswich: Golgonooza Press/Friends of the Centre, 1992).

us, "you plant hope, you plant peace, you plant love, and you will receive God's blessing." Nor did his love of trees remain merely theoretical. When the local farmers came to him for confession, he used to give them as a penance (*epitimion*) the task of planting a tree. His influence has transformed the visible appearance of the island: hillsides which, a hundred years ago, were bare and barren are today thickly covered with pine and eucalyptus.[6]

On the same island of Patmos in September 1995, at an international symposium convened by the Ecumenical Patriarch Bartholomew, as their first and main conclusion the delegates insisted that the misuse of the material creation is to be considered a *sin*. Sins are not just something that we commit against other human beings; we can also sin against the creation. Ecological damage is not due simply to some technical error of judgment, but it is morally and spiritually evil. This is something that Christians have all too often overlooked. What is asked from us is not just greater scientific expertise but nothing less than cosmic repentance.

6. See Kallistos Ware, "Through the Creation to the Creator," *Ecotheology 2* (1997), pp. 8-30, especially pp. 8-9.

CHAPTER 3
APOPHATIC ANTHROPOLOGY

Here, then, are four urgent reasons why in the twenty-first century it is imperative for us to deepen our understanding of human personhood. In doing so, we shall need to be explorers and pioneers; for, alike in the Patristic and Byzantine era and in more recent times, we shall not find anywhere a fully articulated system of Christian anthropology. The Ecumenical Councils were concerned primarily with the dogmas of the Trinity and the Incarnation; and, while the conciliar definitions concerning Triadology and Christology involved at many points presuppositions regarding the nature of the person, yet these presuppositions were not explicitly discussed by the Councils as an issue in its own right. The Councils and the Fathers offer us many precious insights concerning personhood but not a single developed doctrine. In particular, many of the terms applied to the human person, such as *nous* and *dianoia,* have never been precisely defined, and are interpreted by different writers in varying ways. What Archpriest Georges Florovsky used to say about ecclesiology –that it is still *im Werden,* "in the process of formation" – is certainly true also of Christian anthropology.

I hope that, in investigating this little explored field of Christian anthropology, we Orthodox will not attempt to work in isolation. There is much that we can learn from western specialists –philosophers, theologians, social scientists and psychologists – that will deepen our understanding of our own Orthodox tradition. Let us attempt to reach an understanding of human personhood that will be genuinely ecumenical.

Our vision of our own selves, so I believe, needs to be developed in the new millennium pre-eminently in three ways. These can best be summed up in the words mystery, image and mediator:

First, as human beings we are a *mystery* to ourselves.

Second, the decisive element in our human personhood is that we are created in the *image and likeness* of God.

Third, each of us is called to act as priest of the creation and *mediator.*

First, then, as human beings we know and understand only a small part of what we are; we are a mystery to ourselves. Who am I? What am I? The answer is not at all obvious. The bounds of each person are exceedingly wide, overlapping with those of other persons, interpenetrating, ranging over space and time, reaching out of space into infinity and out of time into eternity. We do not know what are the possibilities as yet latent in human personalness, what are the ultimate limits of personhood, what is the true fulfillment of being a person.

However we choose to define personhood –and in contemporary psychology and sociology there is in fact no single, generally agreed definition – it has to be admitted that any such definition is far from being exhaustive. Personhood remains irreducible; its reality cannot simply be deconstructed and reduced to the facts of the appropriate sciences. The actual experience of being a person is far greater than any particular explanation that we choose to give of it; "The heart is deep" (Ps. 63[64]:6). In the words of Thomas Traherne, the seventeeth-century Anglican poet and theologian, we humans are "infinitely mysterious, divine and blessed".

One particular way in which this mysteriousness becomes manifest is in our creativity. The human person is that in which new beginnings are continually being made. By contrast, a computer is not creative. It can do no more than reorganize the material that it is fed into it, thereby disclosing interconnections and consequences of which we were previously unaware; but it does not make new beginnings. The human person, on the other hand, is essentially open, always pointing beyond our present situation to a future as yet unrealized: "Even now we are God's children, but what we will be has not yet been revealed to us" (1 John 3:2). Personhood is in this way a potent sign of hope. To be a human is to be endlessly varied, innovative, unexpected, self-transcending.

The Greek Fathers gave a specific reason for this mysterious, indefinable character of the person. As human beings we are formed in God's image and likeness; since God is incomprehensible, so also is God's image, the human person. In the words of St Gregory of Nyssa, "Has anyone ever understood his own intellect (*nous*)?... An image is only truly such in so far as it expresses the attributes of its archetype. One of the characteristics of Godhead is to be in its essence beyond our understanding; and so the image should also express this,"[7] In our talk about humans, then, as well as in our talk about God, there needs to be an apophatic dimension. Negative theology requires as its counterpart a negative or apophatic anthropology.

---

7. *On the Creation of the Human Being* 11(*PG* 44: 153D, 156B).

CHAPTER 4
LIVING ICON OF THE LIVING GOD

St Gregory's words about archetype and image bring us to our second point. For a Christian, the most decisive single fact about our personhood is that we are created in the image and likeness of God (Gen. 1:26-28). Each of us is nothing less than a living icon of the living God, a created image of God's uncreated infinity. That is why we are free and creative, that is why we reach out beyond space and time, that is why we are "divine and blessed."

Because it is in this way iconic, human nature is inescapably relational. In the very essence of our humanness there is implied a relationship with God, and apart from this relationship our personhood is unintelligible. To be human signifies a sense of direction, a goal, an orientation – an orientation toward God. In the Orthodox understanding of the person, there is no "natural" human being apart from God. Isolated from God, ignoring any relationship with God, humanity is not in a natural but a highly unnatural state. It is a grave error to devise a double-level or "two-storey" doctrine of human nature, first defining the person in terms of itself, as an autonomous, self-contained entity, and only then speaking of our relationship with God as a kind of addendum or appendix. No: our Godward orientation has to be the starting-point of our anthropology, not an afterthought.

As human persons, that is to say, we do not contain our "mystery" exclusively within ourselves. The human being without God is no longer authentically human, but becomes subhuman. We have God as the innermost centre of our being, the determining element in our humanness. As humans we are created for fellowship and communion with God; and if we ignore or repudiate that fellowship and communion, we deny our own true self. Atheism leads to dehumanization, as Josef Stalin's prison camps made only too evident. Affirm the human, and you affirm the Divine also; deny the Divine, and equally you deny the human.

I remember how this point was emphasized by Archimandrite Sophrony (Sakharov), disciple of St Silouan the Athonite and founder of the Monastery of St John the Baptist in Tolleshunt Knights, Essex. At a meeting in Oxford many years ago, as the discussion drew to a close, the chairman said that there was time for just one more question. "Tell me," asked someone in the back row of the audience, "what is God?" Fr. Sophrony briefly replied, "Will you first tell me: what is man?" Yes, indeed: our God-awareness and our human self-awareness are mutually interdependent. If we wish to understand our human identity, let us look at God our archetype; and if we wish to understand God, let us look at the divine image delineated in the mirror of our own heart.

In what particular aspect or faculty of the human person should the divine image be located? This is something that was never precisely defined by any church council; and in fact during the course of Christian history the question has been answered in a variety of ways. For some, it has meant above all the power of reason; for others it has signified kingship over the created order, freedom and creativity. Many Patristic authors, such as St Gregory of Nazianzus, St Gregory of Nyssa, and St Isaac the Syrian, associate the image primarily with the soul. But a significant minority, including St Irenaeus and St Cyril of Alexandria, consider that the image is reflected in the total human being, soul and body together. There is no single, agreed viewpoint. In the words of St Epiphanius of Salamis, "Tradition holds that every human being is in the image of God, but it does not define exactly in what this image consists."[8] This imprecision reflects what was stated earlier

---

8. *Panarion* 70, 3, 1. Compare Kallistos Ware, "'In the Image and Likeness': The Uniqueness of the Human Person," in John T. Chirban, *Personhood:*

about the apophatic dimension of anthropology. Personhood remains elusive and ultimately indefinable.

Rather than attempt to specify too narrowly the scope and character of the divine image, let us hold fast two basic truths. First, "in the image of God" means in the image of Christ the Creator Logos; second, it means in the image of God the Holy Trinity. First, then, in seeking an answer to the question "Who am I? What am I?" we look at Christ; anthropology is a chapter or subdivision of Christology. But in the second place we also understand ourselves in the light of the mutual love of three persons of the Trinity. In the words of the Romanian theologian Dumitru Staniloae, "The Trinity alone assures our existence as persons"; as the Russian Nikolai Fyodorov asserts, "Our social programme is the dogma of the Trinity."[9]

Orthodox Christianity and the Connection between Body, Mind and Soul (Westport, Conn./London: Bergin & Garvey, 1996), pp. 1-13.

9. On this theme, consult Michael Aksionov Meerson, *The Trinity of Love in Modern Russian Theology: The Love Paradigm and the Retrieval of Western Love Mysticism in Modern Russian Trinitarian Thought (from Solovyov to Bulgakov)* (Quincy, Ill.: Franciscan Press, 1998).

CHAPTER 5
PRIEST OF THE CREATION

As a third basic element in our Christian anthropology during the twenty-first century, we need to reactivate the Greek Patristic idea of the human person as mediator between heaven and earth, as cosmic liturgist, as priest of the creation.

To understand our human vocation as mediator and priest, let us take two representative statements from the Fathers, the first from St Gregory of Nazianzus and the second from St Maximus the Confessor.[10] From Clement of Alexandria onward, a long series of Patristic authors describes the human being as *methorios,* "on the border." Such is exactly the approach of Gregory of Nazianzus, even though he does not employ this actual word.[11] The human person, he says, is "a twofold being... earthly yet heavenly, temporal yet immortal, visible yet intelligible." Angels belong to the invisible and spiritual level of reality, animals to the material and physical. Human persons alone belong to the two levels at once, possessing as they do both a material body and an intelligent soul. They do not perhaps stand at the summit of creation – most of the Fathers, although not all, consider that angels occupy a higher level in the hierarchy of being – but, if not at the summit, humans are certainly at the centre and crossroads of the created order. Human nature, precisely because it is mixed – "on the border" between the spiritual and the material – is more complex than the angelic, and by virtue of this greater complexity it possesses richer potentialities.

10. Here I am summarizing points made in my article, "The Unity of the Human Person according to the Greek Fathers," in Arthur Peacocke and Grant Gillett, eds., *Persons and Personality: A Contemporary Inquiry* (Oxford: Basil Blackwell, 1987), pp. 197-206.

11. *Oration* 38:11 (*PG* 36: 321C-324B).

Embracing as we do the full diversity of the creation, each human being is, in Gregory's words, "a second cosmos, a great universe within a little one." Here he deliberately reverses the familiar Hellenic notion of the human being as microcosm. The "great universe" is not the external world, extending though it does for millions of light years through outer space. Incomparably vaster is the inner space of the human heart. We humans are not *microcosmos* but *megalocosmos*.

Yet there is more to be said than this. Made in the image and likeness of God, the human person is not only *microcosmos* and not only *megalocosmos*, but also – far more profoundly and significantly – *microtheos*. As beings formed from both the material and the non-material, we are each *imago mundi*, "image of the world," endowed with the vocation of balancing, reconciling and harmonizing the entire created order in and through ourselves. But, beyond and above this, as *imago Dei*, "image of God," we also have the possibility through divine grace of transcending ourselves and, in and through this act of self-transcendence, of offering the world back to God. Gregory sees human salvation in terms of *theosis*, "deification" or "divinization"; the human being, he says, is *zōon theoumenon*, "an animal that is being deified," a living creature that has received the call to become god. And, in becoming god, we unite the creation with the Creator.

Gregory is not blind to the reality of the fall and of human sin. On the contrary, he emphasizes the fragility and ambivalence of our human condition, placed as we are "midway between majesty and lowliness," to use his own words. We are creatures of infinite potentiality, who in practice all too often tragically fail to realize our opportunities. We are capable of so much, but in practice we achieve so little. Yet, despite our fallenness and failure, we are still in the divine image and still possess the God-given possibility of deification. By virtue of our mixed nature and our creation in the divine image, we can still unite earth and heaven, mediating between the two, making earth heavenly and heaven earthly. Gregory calls this possibility of deification "the culmination of the [human] mystery". His use in this context of the term "mystery" is highly significant. Like Gregory of Nyssa, he sees our human vocation in an apophatic perspective, as a mystery beyond our understanding.

Maximus the Confessor also envisages human personhood in mediatorial terms. Just as for Gregory of Nazianzus we human persons are "earthly yet heavenly [...] visible yet intelligible," so for Maximus we are each of us "a laboratory (*ergasterion*) that contains everything in a comprehensive fashion." By virtue of the complexity of our human nature, at once physical and noetic, we are related to all the extreme points within the created order, and so we are called to "mediate" between all these extremities and to draw them to harmony, "the near with the far, the lower with the higher." The human person is thus, as Maximus puts it, a "natural bond of unity" (*physikos syndesmos).* Yet the human vocation extends even further than this. Not only does God call us to unify the created order within itself, but – bearing as we do the divine image in our hearts – we are called to unite the created with the Uncreated. This we bring to pass, according to Maximus, through the power of love.[12]

Gregory of Nazianzus and Maximus the Confessor do not in any way imagine that human beings can perform this mediating task isolated and unaided by virtue of their own intrinsic powers. On the contrary, such mediation is possible only in and through Christ

---

12. *Ambigua* 41 (*PG* 91: 1304D-1308C).

the *Theanthropos* (God-man). It is he, the Second Adam, completely divine and completely human, who constitutes the one true mediator. It is he who holds all things in unity (Col. 1:17) and who gathers and sums them up, "recapitulating them all in himself" (Eph. 1:10). It is only through and in him, by virtue of his incarnation, cross and resurrection, that we humans can act as the mediating bond and bridge of the creation. Deification means Christification.[13]

Here, then, is a theological understanding of human personhood that can guide and inspire us in the twenty-first century as we wrestle with the thorny problems of bioethics and ecology, and as we come to terms with multicultural pluralism. Summing up the implications of what Gregory and Maximus mean when they present the human being as microcosm and mediator, we may say that the human animal is not primarily a logical animal, nor yet a political animal, but much more fundamentally a eucharistic animal.[14] Our highest privilege, our supreme vocation, the act which makes us authentically ourselves, is to offer back the world in thanksgiving to God: "Thine own from Thine own we offer unto Thee, in all things and for all things." Rather than speak of ourselves as kings or stewards of the created world, we should see ourselves as priests of the creation, as offerers and liturgists. Yet this cosmic priesthood can only be exercised through the grace of Jesus Christ, the unique High Priest.[15]

13. For a powerful development of this theme, see Panagiotis Nellas, *Deification in Christ: Orthodox Perspectives on the Nature of the Human Person* (Crestwood, N.Y.: St Vladimir's Seminary Press, 1987), chapter 1.

14. Compare Christos Yannaras in *The Freedom of Morality* (Crestwood, N.Y.: St Vladimir's Seminary Press, 1984), especially chapters 5 and 6.

15. On this, see Fr Alexander Schmemann, *For the Life of the World: Sacra-*

Offering, however, signifies sacrifice; and our analysis of the human vocation will be seriously unbalanced if we fail to allow for this. As the late Ecumenical Patriarch Dimitrios insisted, in his Christmas message of 1989 concerning the ecological crisis, what we need to display is a "eucharistic and ascetic spirit." These two things, Eucharist and asceticism, belong together. In a fallen world, marred by sin, there can be no effective act of thanksgiving without voluntary self-denial. In order to be a eucharistic animal, the human person has also to be an ascetic animal.

By asceticism Patriarch Dimitrios did not of course mean simply rules about fasting and the number of prostrations that we make during our prayer, although these certainly have a place in our ascetic struggle, in our *podvig*. Much more fundamentally he had in view an attitude of self-restraint, of kenotic simplicity in our total life-style, a willingness to distinguish, both as communities and on a personal level, between what we *want* and what we *need*. Because we want something, it does not automatically follow that we are entitled to have it. This is a lesson that affluent societies throughout the world are unwilling to learn. In a word, Patriarch Dimitrios meant a spirit of costly sacrifice. As his successor the Ecumenical Patriarch Bartholomew rightly emphasized in his address at the great ecological assembly in Venice on 10 June 2002, sacrifice is precisely the "missing dimension" in our present-day ecological outlook.[16]

---

ments and Orthodoxy, revised edition (Crestwood, N.Y.: St Vladimir's Seminary Press, 1988), especially pp. 60-61; Paulos Gregorios, *The Human Presence: An Orthodox View of Nature* (Geneva: WCC, 1978), especially pp. 82-89.

16. The full text of Patriarch Bartholomew's address, "Sacrifice: The Missing Dimension," can be found in John Chryssavgis, *Cosmic, Grace, Humble Prayer: The Ecological Vision of the Green Patriarch Bartholomew I* (Grand Rapids, Mich.: Eerdmans, 2003).

In the Divine Liturgy thanksgiving and offering, Eucharist and sacrifice, are so closely linked together that they constitute a single reality, an undivided action. So it has also to be throughout our whole human life, in "the Liturgy after the Liturgy." We cannot be genuinely eucharistic animals, true priests of the creation, unless we are cross-bearers, sharing in the sacrificial self-offering of Christ our great High Priest; unless, that is to say, we lay down our lives in generous love, dying that others may live. Perfect love is sacrificial love. "Offer the world back to God in thanksgiving" means "Offer your own life in sacrifice to God, for the sake of your fellow-humans." Yet such sacrifice, so we shall discover, brings us not loss but gain. *Kenosis* leads to *plerosis,* self-emptying brings self-fulfilment. As our Lord Himself has assured us, if we lose our life for his sake we shall save it (Matt. 10:39). In the words of C. S. Lewis, "Nothing that you have not given away will really be yours."[17]

Here, then, are three elements – mystery, image, mediator – that, as I believe, will prove central in our anthropological explorations within the multicultural pluralism of the new millennium. There are doubtless other themes, besides these three, that could and should be added; human personhood, as we have already noted, is inexhaustible.

Whatever our choice of dominant issues, there is certainly one underlying element that is fundamental to any understanding of human personhood, and that is the quality of love. Without love we are not human. It is love that lies at the heart of the human mystery, love that expresses the Christological and Trinitarian image within us, love that enables us to act as priests of the creation

17. *Mere Christianity*, (London: Harper Collins, 1977), p. 189.

and mediators. During the early part of the seventeenth century, inaugurating a fresh era in philosophy, René Descartes chose as his point of departure the principle *Cogito, ergo sum*, "I think, therefore I am." He might have done better – since the human animal is far more than simply an animal that thinks – to have taken as his starting-point the affirmation *Amo, ergo sum*, "I love, therefore I am"; or, better still, *Amor, ergo sum*, "I am loved, therefore I am." In the words of Fr Dimitru Staniloae, "If I am not loved, I am unintelligible to myself."[18] As Paul Evdokimov states, the greatest event between God and the human person – and we may add, between one human person and another – is to love and to be loved.[19] If we can make love the starting-point and the end-point in our doctrine of personhood, our Christian witness in the twenty-first century will prove altogether creative and life-giving.

---

18. Marc-Antoine Costa de Beauregard, *Dumitru Staniloae: Ose Comprendre que je t'aime* (Paris: Cerf, 1983), p. 24.

19. *Sacrement de l'amour* (Paris: Éditions de l'Épi, 1962), p. 79; tr. Antony P. Gythiel and Victoria Steadman, *The Sacrament of Love: The Nuptial Mystery in the Light of the Orthodox Tradition* (Crestwood, N.Y.: St Vladimir's Seminary Press, 1985), p. 59. Evdokimov is citing Kallistos Kataphygiotes.

INDEX